Although every effort has been made to ensure that website addresses are correct at time of going to press, Hodder Education cannot be held responsible for the content of any website mentioned in this book. It is sometimes possible to find a relocated web page by typing in the address of the home page for a website in the URL window of your browser.

Hachette UK's policy is to use papers that are natural, renewable and recyclable products and made from wood grown in well-managed forests and other controlled sources. The logging and manufacturing processes are expected to conform to the environmental regulations of the country of origin.

To order, please visit www.hoddereducation.com or contact Customer Service at education@hachette.co.uk / +44 (0)1235 827827.

ISBN: 978 1 0360 0699 0

© Richard Howe 2024

First published in 2024 by Hodder Education (a trading division of Hodder & Stoughton Limited),
An Hachette UK Company
Carmelite House
50 Victoria Embankment
London EC4Y 0DZ

www.hoddereducation.com

The authorised representative in the EEA is Hachette Ireland, 8 Castlecourt Centre, Dublin 15, D15 XTP3, Ireland (email: info@hbgi.ie)

Impression number 10 9 8 7 6 5 4 3 2

Year   2028 2027 2026 2025

All rights reserved. Apart from any use permitted under UK copyright law, no part of this publication may be reproduced or transmitted in any form or by any means, electronic or mechanical, including photocopying and recording, or held within any information storage and retrieval system, without permission in writing from the publisher or under licence from the Copyright Licensing Agency Limited. Further details of such licences (for reprographic reproduction) may be obtained from the Copyright Licensing Agency Limited, www.cla.co.uk

Cover photo © Seventyfour – stock.adobe.com

Illustrations by Integra, India

Typeset in India

Printed in the UK

A catalogue record for this title is available from the British Library.

Contents

1 **Problem solving**   4

2 **Introduction to programming**   13

3 **Emerging issues and impact of digital**   28

4 **Legislation and regulatory requirements**   38

5 **Business context**   50

6 **Data**   61

7 **Digital environments**   71

8 **Security**   87

Answers can be found online at hoddereducation.com/answers-and-extras

1 Problem solving

Recall activities

1   Complete the table by writing three key aspects of each problem-solving approach.

Problem-solving approach		
Top-down	Bottom-up	Modularisation
1	1	1
2	2	2
3	3	3

2   Match each key term to its definition by drawing a line between them.

Key term
Decomposition
Abstraction
Algorithm

Definition
Set of instructions that describe a solution to a problem
Breaking down a complex problem into manageable component parts
Extracting key details from a problem and ignoring irrelevant information

3   Explain two advantages of using algorithms.

1 ....

2 ....

4   Explain two disadvantages of using algorithms.

1 ....

2 ....

5   List the four standard arithmetic expressions.

1 ....

2 ....

3 ....

4 ....

6 Complete the table about relational operators.

Symbol	Description	Example
	Equal to or equivalent	y = 7
<>		x <> 6
	Greater than	
>=		
	Less than	y < 4
<=	Less than OR equal to	

7 Solve the clues to complete the crossword.

Across
3 Use of standard shapes to produce a diagram of the features of an algorithm
8 Description of an algorithm using a mix of programming terminology and informal notation
10 Instructions in a code, executed in order
11 Formal structure of statements in programming

Down
1 Sequence of instructions that perform a specific task, grouped together in one unit
2 Put a data set in a specific order
4 Tool used to test for logical errors when an algorithm or program executes
5 Code executed when a condition is met
6 Statement in an algorithm leading to different actions based on a True/False answer
7 Instructions that are repeated for a set number of times
9 Examine data to find a defined value

Short-answer exam-style practice questions

1 Explain the term 'computational thinking'. (1 mark)

　..

2 Explain how modularisation can simplify the solving of complex problems. (2 marks)

　..

　..

> **Hint**
> The first mark is for defining the key term 'modularisation'. The second mark is for explaining how this impacts the question context.

3 Explain the purpose of using a trace table. (2 marks)

　..

　..

4 Written descriptions and program code are two methods of writing an algorithm.

　Explain one other method of writing an algorithm. (2 marks)

　..

　..

5 Explain the difference between constants and variables. (2 marks)

　..

　..

6 Explain how a decision is constructed in a flowchart algorithm. (4 marks)

　..

　..

　..

　..

　..

　..

Long-answer exam-style practice questions

1 Below is the pseudocode for an algorithm.
```
 1 Set Mark to 0
 2 RECEIVE Mark FROM (INTEGER) KEYBOARD
 3 IF Mark > 65 THEN
 4 DISPLAY "Well done you gained a Distinction"
 5 ELSEIF Mark >45 AND <66 THEN
 6 DISPLAY "Well done you gained a Merit"
 7 ELSEIF Mark >35 AND <45 THEN
 8 DISPLAY "Well done you gained a Pass"
 9 ELSEIF Mark <36
10 Display "Sorry, you need to retake the test"
11 ENDIF
```

Describe what this algorithm does. (3 marks)

> **Hint**
> 'Describe' means tell the examiner what happens. This question has 3 marks, so think about three things that happen one after the other – like three steps in the sand.

....

....

....

....

....

2 By referring to the algorithm in question 1, complete the table with answers that will be displayed on screen when the marks are entered. (3 marks)

Mark entered	Message displayed on screen
72	
28	
47	

3 Explain how an error will be thrown up by the code in question 1 and state one way in which it could be corrected. (4 marks)

....

....

....

....

> **Hint**
>
> This question is asking about an issue with an algorithm and how to solve it. There are four marks, so you need to make four points.
>
> Step 1: find the error and explain the effect.
>
> Step 2: say why this happens.
>
> Step 3: state what needs to be changed to correct the error.
>
> Step 4: say how this solves the problem.

> **Sample answer**
>
> If 45 is entered, then the value is not accepted (1 mark) in the code as it is set to < or > 45, but not equal to 45. (1 mark)
>
> Line 5 (1 mark) could be edited to >= (1 mark) 45 if 45 is allowed for a Merit
>
> OR
>
> Line 7 (1 mark) could be edited to <=45 (1 mark) if 45 is pass grade.
>
> **Comment**
>
> The first part of the question requires finding the error in the algorithm. When looking at the algorithm, there is an issue with number 45 because the code only allows greater than or less than 45. This means that a mark of 45 would not be accepted.
>
> Once this is explained, then the algorithm needs to be fixed, by altering one line of code to accept the value of 45. If *both* of the lines with errors are altered, it would cause another issue with the program not knowing what to do with a mark of 45.

4 A local car hire company uses a computer system to calculate customers fees.

The cost of a journey during the day is £4 for the first mile and £3 for every additional mile. If there are more than three passengers in the taxi, an extra 50% is added to the fare.

Write an algorithm in pseudocode to calculate the cost of a day-time journey.

The algorithm must:

▷ allow the user to enter the number of passengers and journey as whole numbers

▷ calculate the cost of the journey

▷ output the final calculated journey cost on a screen to show the customer. (7 marks)

1 Problem solving

Plan your own answer

To start solving the problem, decompose it (break it down into parts or modules). The table walks you through the steps you need to take to answer question 4. A sample answer is shown overleaf.

Points to consider	Possible answers (try writing the pseudocode)
How will the number of passengers and distances be entered into the program?	
Is the journey more than 1 mile? If so, how will you calculate that distance?	
How much do any extra miles cost? How will you calculate this?	
Add the cost of these extra miles to the cost of the first mile.	
What question needs to be asked about the number of passengers? What happens if the answer is true? What happens to the cost of the journey as a total?	
What is the final cost of the journey in the question?	
How is the final cost shown to the customer?	

> **Sample answer**
>
> RECEIVE Distance FROM (REAL) KEYBOARD
>
> RECEIVE Passengers FROM (REAL) KEYBOARD
>
> ExtraDistance = Distance – 1
>
> CostOfExtraDistance = ExtraDistance * 3
>
> FinalCost = 4 + CostOfExtraDistance
>
> IF Passengers >3 THEN
>
>   Surcharge = FinalCost / 2
>
> FinalCost = FinalCost + Surcharge
>
> ENDIF
>
> SEND 'FinalCost' TO DISPLAY
>
> **Comment**
>
> At the start of the answer the methods used to input the data into the system are stated and names for the data are given. (1 mark)
>
> Then the lowest level calculations are developed – calculating the extra miles above the first mile (1 mark), followed by how much these extra miles will cost. (1 mark)
>
> Then the cost of the extra miles needs to be added to the cost of the first mile, which is different in value. (1 mark)
>
> That provides all the mileage costs, but there is also an extra charge (surcharge) if there are more than three passengers. So, this needs an IF statement that calculates if there are more than three passengers. (1 mark)
>
> If there are more than three, then the distance cost needs to be halved (1 mark) and added onto the distance cost to provide a final total cost which is displayed on the screen. (1 mark, 7 marks in total)
>
> Now write the final pseudocode in the space on the previous page. Have you covered everything?

5 In a sports league, the scores for each team are input into a computer which updates the points for each team.

   ▷ If a match is drawn, both teams get 1 point each.

   ▷ If a team wins a match, it gets 3 points.

   ▷ If a team loses a match, it gets 0 points.

This is an algorithm for updating the points for a drawn match between Team X and Team Y:

```
IF TeamXGoals = TeamYGoals THEN
TeamXPoints = TeamXPoints + 1
TeamYPoints = TeamYPoints + 1
ENDIF
```

At the top of the next page, draw a flow chart for updating the points if one of the teams wins their match against the other team. (6 marks)

6 A software development company is designing a new health tracker app for mobile devices. They are using a modularisation approach to the development of the app.

Discuss the benefits and drawbacks of using this approach. (9 marks)

7 In pseudocode, write a program that converts a dog's age into the equivalent human age.

The program must include the following:

▷ User input using a keyboard for the dog's age in whole years only.

▷ Convert the dog's age by:

   ▷ multiplying the age by 12 and then adding 31 if the dog's age is 2 or less

   ▷ multiplying the age by 16 and then adding 31 if the dog's age is more than 2.

▷ Output the initial dog and human equivalent on printed paper. (6 marks)

2 Introduction to programming

Recall activities

1. Complete the table to describe different data types and give examples.

Data type	Description	Example	Real-world example
String			
Character			
Integer			
Real/float			
Boolean			

2. Define the following terms.

   Constant ....

   Variable ....

   Declare ....

   Cast ....

3. Complete the following sentences.

   A data structure is a way of .... and storing data on the computer, so it can be .... and modified efficiently. There are .... types of data structures:

   ▷ lists

   ▷ arrays

   ▷ dictionaries

   A .... is an ordered data structure that uses a single .... and an .... It has no predefined .... and does not require defined ....

   An array is a data structure that uses a .... identifier and .... indices to store data. It can be one-dimensional or .... using .... indices. An array has a predefined scope and can .... hold data of the .... data type.

   A dictionary is an ordered data structure that stores the data in a .... of a .... and a .... The .... can be returned by referring to its .... Items in the dictionary can be changed and .... are .... allowed.

4 What is the difference between a local and a global variable?

   ....

5 What is a mathematical operator used for?

   ....

6 What is a relational operator used for?

   ....

7 What is a Boolean operator used for?

   ....

8 Complete the table about operators.

Operator	Purpose	Example of use
==		
<		
>		
<>		
<=		
>=		
NOT		
AND		
OR		

9 Explain each of the following text file opening methods.

"r" ....

"a" ....

"w" ....

"x" ....

10 What does "t" mean?

....

11 What code is used for binary mode in Python?

....

12 Write the Python code for opening and reading a text file called "mynotes".

....

13 Write the pseudocode for opening and reading a text file called "mynotes".

....

14 What is the purpose of the following selection commands?

IF ....

THEN ....

ELSE ....

ELSEIF ....

CASE ....

15 What does a WHILE loop do?

....

16 Why would you use a FOR loop?

....

17 Summarise how each of the following searching algorithms works.

Linear search ....

....

Binary search ....

....

18 Complete the table by listing two benefits and two limitations for each of the sorting algorithms.

	Bubble sort	Insertion sort	Merge sort	Selection sort	Quick sort
Benefit 1					
Benefit 2					
Limitation 1					
Limitation 2					

19 Draw lines to match each validation check to its definition and a matching example.

Validation check
Presence check
Length check
Type check
Format check
Range check
Check digit

Definition
The correct type of data has been entered
Checks data has been entered in a required field
Used to check data has been received properly
Data must be in a specific format
Data can only contain a specified number of characters
Value must be within a range of set values

Example
Number of a barcode
Surname when registering for a driving licence
Age as an integer not text
Number of bags for holiday between 0 and 2
Email address must contain an @ symbol
Phone number

20 Solve the clues to complete the crossword about testing.

Across
3 Testing using market research to understand the strengths and weaknesses of an idea
6 Testing of the interface between two software components
7 Testing individual components in isolation, also known as 'white box' testing
10 Testing the speed, response time and reliability of a software are all examples of this type of testing
12 The number of 'whys' used in a problem-solving method
14 Testing carried out using specialised tools to control how the tests are performed

Down
1 Benefit of software testing in which the product can be trusted to perform properly
2 Three-letter acronym for testing, used to solve problems
4 Name given to testing performed by real users of an application in a real environment
5 Testing to ensure software works on different devices
8 Incorrect data used in testing
9 Testing of the system carried out by the end user to check it meets their requirements
11 Often called 'black box' testing, the product is tested as a whole regardless of the performance of the different elements
13 Correct data used when testing a digital product

Short-answer exam-style practice questions

1   A teacher is developing a program to track the performance of their students as they complete their coursework.

   a Identify the most suitable data types for storing the following. (4 marks)

   Candidate number ....

   Candidate name ....

   Planning phase complete ....

   Final mark ....

   b Explain what an array is. (2 marks)

   ....

   ....

   c Describe what lines 1 to 9 of the code do. (4 marks)

```python
1  def award_grade(mark):
2      if mark > 80:
3          return "Distinction"
4      elif mark > 60:
5          return "Merit"
6      elif mark > 35:
7          return "Pass"
8      else:
9          return "Fail"
10
11
12 student_mark = float(input("Enter the student's mark: "))
13 result = award_grade(student_mark)
14 print(f"The student's result is: {result}")
15
```

   ....

   ....

   ....

   ....

   d Name the process visible between lines 2 and 9. (1 mark)

   ....

2 **Introduction to programming**

2 A game developer is creating a new role-playing game using an electronic dice. Each player gets three goes with the dice before they lose their turn. Each roll of the dice is added together to get the player's score.

```python
import random

def roll_dice():

    return random.randint(1, 6)

def main():

    total_turns = 3


    total_score = 0

    for turn in range(1, total_turns + 1):
        input(f"Press Enter to roll the dice (Turn {turn}/{total_turns}): ")


        result = roll_dice()
        print(f"The dice rolled: {result}")


        total_score += result

        print(f"Player's total score: {total_score}\n")

    print(f"Final score: {total_score}")

if __name__ == "__main__":
    main()

```

a What does the program do in line 1? (2 marks)

....

....

> **Hint**
>
> This question is asking what a specific line of code does.
> - Your first task is to find the code. It is in line 1, using the numbering on the left.
> - Now deconstruct it – the code on line 1 is made up of two words.
> - Explaining what each word means when put together should give you full marks, as there are two marks available.

b Describe how the code counts the number of turns taken by the player. (3 marks)

....

....

....

....

....

c Describe how the code adds together the numbers on the dice to provide a final score for the player. (3 marks)

....

....

....

....

....

d The developer has added in the following code to the program.

What does this code do in the program? (3 marks)

```
24
25          if turn == 2:
26              total_score -= 1
27          elif turn == 3:
28              total_score += 2
29
30          print(f"Player's total score: {total_score}\n")
31
```

....

....

....

....

....

2 Introduction to programming

3 A soft toy manufacturer is creating a new system to store orders.

```
1    animals = ["lion", "bear", "dog", "whale", "seal", "wolf"]
2
3    for x in animals :
4        if x == "dog" :
5            break
6        print ( x )
7
8
```

   a Define the purpose of the code in line 1. (2 marks)

   ....

   ....

   b Explain what this FOR loop does. (4 marks)

   ....

   ....

   ....

   ....

   c Describe what would happen if line 4 is edited to read:

      if x == "wolf" (2 marks)

   ....

   ....

4 A new app is being developed for monitoring a conservatory in the summer.

```
1    def RoomControl (thermo):
2        if thermo < 19:
3            print (thermo, "The room is too cold, close the window and switch the fan off")
4        elif thermo > 26:
5            print (thermo, "The room is too hot, open a window and turn the fan on")
6        else:
7            print(" The room is at the correct temperature")
```

   a Identify the name of the function in the app. (1 mark)

   ....

   b Write the line of Python code that would call this function in a full program. (1 mark)

   ....

5   A shipping company is having issues with its new software that customers use to book and pay for shipping parcels.

These are the criteria for calculating the cost of shipping:

▷ If parcels are under 200 g in weight they cost £3.00 to send.

▷ If they are more than 500 g in weight they cost £8.00 to send.

▷ Between these weights, the price is £5.00 to send.

```
if ParcelWeight == 200:
    print (ParcelWeight, "The shipping cost will be £50.0")
elif ParcelWeight == 500:
    print (ParcelWeight,"The shipping cost will be £8.00")
else:
    print("The shipping cost will be £3.00")
```

a   Identify the issues with the code provided. (4 marks)

b   Write improved code that would solve the issues you identified. (3 marks)

Long-answer exam-style practice questions

1   A local car hire company uses an old computer system to calculate customers fees. They have commissioned a new application to be developed by an IT company.

Evaluate the importance of using compatibility testing when developing this new software. (9 marks)

2 Introduction to programming

....
....
....
....
....

> **Plan your own answer**
>
> To start solving the problem, decompose it (break it down into parts). The table walks you through the steps you need to take to answer question 1.
>
> | Points to consider | Possible answers |
> |---|---|
> | What is compatibility testing? | |
> | What could be tested? | |
> | Why would these be tested? | |
> | How do these link to the hire company's system? | |
> | How important is it to carry out this form of testing? | |
> | What happens if you don't do this type of testing? | |

> **Sample answer**
>
> Compatibility testing is making sure that the application will work in a range of situations. This could include the use of different hardware and operating systems. It could also be concerned with different connectivity methods and browsers.
>
> The application could be used on a desktop computer which is operating Windows. The company needs to test that the application will work on this device configuration. The hire company may use an Apple computer, so the application needs to work on this device as well. This will mean that the application will need to be tested on an Apple device with its specific OS.
>
> **Comment**
>
> The student has explained what compatibility testing is and what could be tested. The answer identifies the context of the question and identifies hardware that the hire company could have. This means that the IT company would need to test the application using these device configurations.
>
> This is a good start which can then be developed further to include other aspects that could be tested in the context. Finally, you would need to explain why the use of compatibility testing is important.

2 The new application in question 1 uses pre-written code.

Evaluate why pre-written code might be used by the IT company. (9 marks)

> **Plan your own answer**
>
> To start solving the problem, decompose it (break it down into parts). The table walks you through the steps you need to take to answer question 2.
>
> | Points to consider | Possible answers |
> |---|---|
> | What is pre-written code? | |
> | What are its benefits? | |
> | What are its drawbacks? | |
> | Where would you *not* use it? | |
> | Why might it be used in this development? | |
>
> Now use the information from the table to answer question 2.

....
....
....
....
....
....
....
....
....
....
....
....
....
....
....

3 As the new application for the local hire company in question 1 has been developed, beta testing has been carried out.

Explain the importance of carrying out beta testing as part of application development. (9 marks)

....

....

....

....

....

....

....

....

....

> **Hint**
>
> In this answer, consider who does the beta testing and what they might say as a result of the testing. Then consider how this information could be used to finalise the application.

4 Explain how the use of root cause analysis could be used to deal with the loss of stored customer data. (9 marks)

....

....

....

....

....

....

....

....

....

5 An online shopping website requires customers to create an account.

Evaluate the importance of implementing a range of validation techniques when developing the account-creation part of the website. (9 marks)

....

....

....

....

....

....

....

....

....

....

....

....

6 Evaluate how the use of a poorly constructed test plan when developing a new application can cause issues with the final application. (9 marks)

....

....

....

....

....

....

....

....

....

....

....

....

7 A new social media application is being developed by a team of developers working remotely. Evaluate the suitability of comments in Python when developing the application. (9 marks)

3 Emerging issues and impact of digital

Recall activities

1 Complete the table by defining the terms.

Term	Definition
Cultural	
Ethical	
Moral	
Social	
Societal norms	

2 a List four things that an acceptable use policy (AUP) could cover.

1 .... 3 ....

2 .... 4 ....

b List four other internal organisational policies.

1 .... 3 ....

2 .... 4 ....

3 Complete the table to consider how the use of digital technology has impacted on some aspects of our lives. Provide an example of a positive impact and a negative impact for each aspect.

	Positive impact	Negative impact
Changes in societal norm		
Changes in cultures in organisations		
Environmental issues		
Globalisation		
Inclusion and diversity		

4 List two aims of a professional organisation.

1 ....

2 ....

5 Match each technique with its definition by drawing a line between them.

Techniques	Definition
Observing normal behaviour	Being aware of what is going on around you, including people, buildings and events
Awareness of co-workers	Notice the behaviour and emotions of others around you and how this may differ from their norm
Situational awareness	Establishing a person's regular pattern of work by watching them in the working environment

6 Solve the clues to complete the crossword about emerging trends and technologies.

Across
2 The IoT is made up of four of these
6 The imitation of the workings of the human brain by a machine
7 What does IoT means?
8 An immersive technology placing the user fully in an alternative situation

Down
1 One part of the IoT that use wearable devices
3 The superimposing of digital content on a real-world view
4 What is generated by wearable devices
5 The calculations carried out in the cloud and another part of the IoT
9 Computer systems that perform tasks normally requiring human intelligence

Digital Production, Design and Development T Level Exam Practice Workbook

Short-answer exam-style practice questions

1 A new app for monitoring people's health is being developed. The app will provide guidance on how people can maintain and improve their health. The designers of the app need to research into how people look after their health.

   Give three levels of situation awareness that will be required when carrying out the research. (3 marks)

   ....

   ....

   ....

2 Discuss how machine learning could be used with the new health app and how it could impact the app's effectiveness. (4 marks)

   ....

   ....

   ....

   ....

   ....

   > **Hint**
   >
   > The first part of this response should define what machine learning is. The second part should talk about how it can affect the app, in terms of learning about users' behaviours. The final part of the answer is to explain how that will impact on the app and make it more effective.

3 Explain how AR can be used to train new crane operators. (3 marks)

   ....

   ....

   ....

4 Explain how automotive processes can be used by a supermarket to manage their stock. (4 marks)

   ....

   ....

   ....

   ....

5 a Describe open-source software. (2 marks)

....

....

....

....

b Explain two disadvantages of using open-source software when developing an app. (4 marks)

....

....

....

....

6 Identify the purpose of a strategic plan when setting up a new company. (3 marks)

....

....

....

....

7 Explain why an organisation may develop a social media policy for their workers. (3 marks)

....

....

....

....

8 Describe one negative impact of an organisation monitoring its employees. (2 marks)

....

....

....

....

Long-answer exam-style practice questions

1 Discuss the impact of digital technologies on the environment. (9 marks)

> **Plan your own answer**
>
> To start solving the problem, decompose it (break it down into parts). The first table defines the terms used in question 1. The second table will help you construct your answer.
>
> | Key words in the question | How these relate to the question and your answer |
> |---|---|
> | Discuss | 'Discuss' means talking about both sides of the issue, so give positive and negative impacts. You will also need to give a conclusion. |
> | Impact | The 'impacts' are the effects, how things have changed, both positively and negatively. |
> | Digital technologies | The digital technologies in the specification are AI, VR, AR, and automated processes. |
> | Environment | This refers to the places where we live and the planet as a whole. |
>
> Copy and complete the second table, summarising the points you will cover in your answer. One impact has been done for you. Remember to cover both negative and positive impacts.
>
> | Points to cover | Impact |
> |---|---|
> | Increased mining of rare resources | Negative impact – landscape being altered and depleted due to increased demand for minerals and metals needed in digital technologies. |
> | | |
> | | |
> | | |
> | | |
> | Conclusion | |
>
> Now write your answer to question 1, using the information you have planned in the table.

....

....

....

....

....

....

....

....

3 Emerging issues and impact of digital

....
....
....
....
....
....
....

2 A new health app will collect the user's personal information and track their movements.

Evaluate the legal and ethical issues that will need to be addressed. (12 marks)

Plan your own answer

To start solving the problem, decompose it (break it down into parts). The first table will help you define the terms used in question 2. The second table will help you construct your answer.

Key words in the question	How these relate to the question and your answer
Evaluate	'Evaluate' means looking at the impacts of the issues. What are the issues and impacts here, and how can they be addressed?
Legal issues	Based on your knowledge of legislation, what are the legal considerations? What data is being collected? Is it sensitive data? What will this mean for the design of the app?
Ethical issues	Who has access to the data? Who could use the data? Legally are they allowed? Remember, app users have privacy rights and the right to live their lives as they want.
User data	What data is collected: steps, heart rate, personal details, how much the app user moves and how much they sit? Other lifestyle choices?

Copy and complete the second table, summarising the points you will cover in your answer. One issue has been done for you. Remember to cover both negative and positive impacts.

Points to cover	Impact
Personal data is collected when creating an account	Legally, data needs to be protected based on the Data Protection Act, 2018. Specific security will need to be used to protect the data. Data can only be used for specific purposes and only specific people can see it.

Now write your answer to question 2 on the lines over the page, using the information you have planned in the table.

Sample answer

The health app will collect a range of data about the user. Some of this data is classified as personal and sensitive data. This means that the data will be covered by the Data Protection Act, 2018, which governs the legal precautions that must be put in place to protect the use and storage of this data. When signing up for the app, the user will need to input personal data such as name, address and age. All this data must be stored and used in compliance with the Data Protection Act. This places a burden on the app developer to ensure that adequate security protocols are in place, reducing the chances of the data being accessed in an unauthorised way.

When installing the app and signing up, the user must know and accept the terms of use. This will include information about how the data will be used and who will have access it. This is another example of how the app developer must comply with the legal requirements of the Data Protection Act. It also causes an ethical issue regarding who will have access to the data. The app developers may ask users to give permission to pass the data onto other organisations. This could include health insurance companies. If the app user grants permission, legally their data can be passed on to other organisations, but it creates an ethical issue of whether these companies should have access to personal data. Insurance companies could use this information to assess insurance cover on the individual. They can also use this information when designing policies to create 'profiles' of types of people based on activity levels.

Another ethical issue is that the health app will be tracking people continually and could make the user feel that they are being monitored. This could cause some users to remove the app and be lost as a customer. To deal with this, the app developer should consider how they can provide the user with ways of turning off the monitoring of activity.

The app developer would need to consider both the legal and ethical issues that would impact on the user of the app. Some of these would directly impact the app and some indirectly, in relation to who has access to the data.

Comment

The student starts off by talking about what data will be collected in the app and so sets the scene with the legal issues that need to be addressed. As the app user's personal data is collected, the answer links this to the relevant legislation and how that will impact the app developers. The answer also talks about the ethical issue of how the app developer can pass information on to other parties. The legal aspect is briefly covered by talking about gaining permission from the user, and then how an ethical issue is created by the types of companies that can access the data, in this case insurance companies.

The response shows a good analysis of some of the points and links them to the context of the health app. Two ethical issues are covered but these could be expanded. The legal issues need to be covered in greater depth to achieve the higher levels of the mark scheme.

There is a basic conclusion which would need to be developed for higher marks. So, while the answer starts off well and covers a range of points, this response would only gain marks in the middle mark band.

Now try to develop an expanded answer that would gain higher marks.

3 Discuss the use of virtual reality to train road maintenance workers before they work on motorway repairs. (9 marks)

4 Evaluate how the Internet of Things (IoT) can be used by a restaurant to improve their business efficiency. (9 marks)

5 Discuss how the development of a new digital system for monitoring staff performance must consider legal and ethical issues. (9 marks)

4 Legislation and regulatory requirements

Recall activities

1. List the four actions that employers must complete to ensure the safety of their workers when using computer systems.

   1 ....
   2 ....
   3 ....
   4 ....

2. Label the diagram to show how a workstation can be made safe for work.

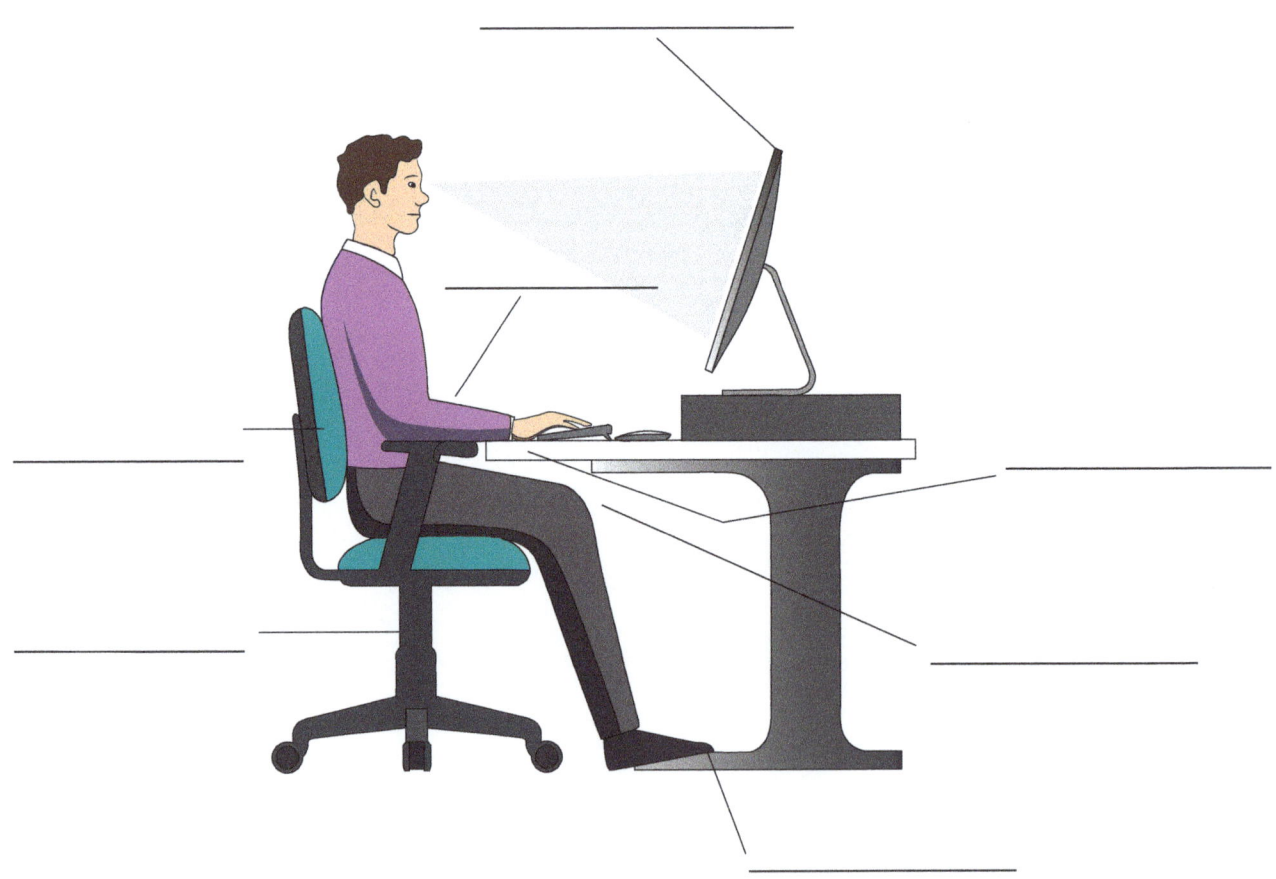

3 Complete the table by describing each term.

Term	Description
Information Commissioner's Office	
Data subject	
Personal data	
Data controller	
Opt in/opt out	

4 Summarise each principle of the Data Protection Act, 2018.

1 ....

2 ....

3 ....

4 ....

5 ....

6 ....

7 ....

8 ....

5 Link each section of the Computer Misuse Act, 1990, with its offence and penalty by drawing a line between them.

Section
1
2
3
3A
3ZA

Offence
Unauthorised modification of data
Unauthorised access to computer material
Unauthorised acts leading to serious risk or damage
Unauthorised access with intent to commit further crime
Making, supplying or obtaining any articles for use maliciously on a computer

Penalty
Unlimited fine and up to 5 years in prison
Unlimited fine and up to 14 years in prison
Maximum fine of £5000 and up to 6 months in prison
Unlimited fine and/or up to 5 years in prison
Unlimited fine and/or up to 5 years in prison

6 Solve the clues to complete the crossword.

Across

2 Software used to record the keys pressed on a keyboard by a worker
3 US legislation governing the digital systems used for electronic communications
6 Granted to the owner of a design to stop others making, using or selling it for a specified period of time
8 Article 8 of this protects a person's private correspondence
9 Uses satellites to track employees' vehicles when delivering goods

Down

1 I .... Property Act, 2014
4 Used to watch a location
5 Electronic .... can be used to monitor access to locations in a building
7 Location covered by the Digital Services Act, 2022

4 Legislation and regulatory requirements

7 Complete the diagram by listing the protected characteristics in the Equality Act, 2010.

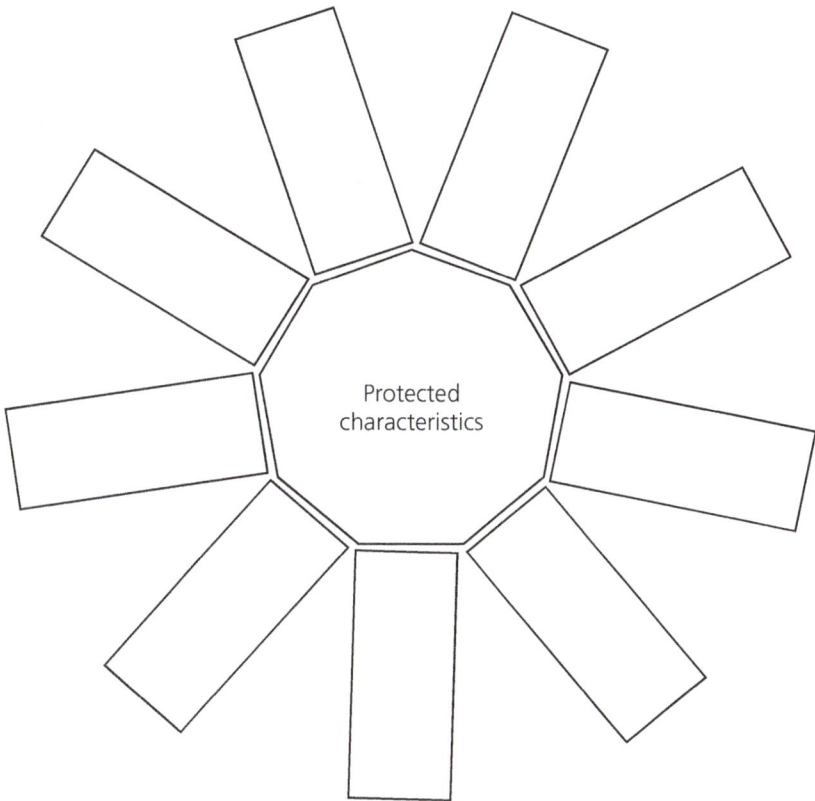

8 Complete the following sentences.

  a The organisation responsible for the developing web standards is

  ....

  ....

  (............................).

  b The organisation responsible for setting standards for the architecture of the internet is the

  ....

  ....

  (............................).

  c .... is a set of rules used to transfer files using the internet.

9 For each principle of the web content accessibility guidelines (WCAG), write a definition and give two examples of the principle in use.

  a Perceivable

  Definition ....

  Example 1 ....

  Example 2 ....

b Operable

Definition ....

Example 1 ....

Example 2 ....

c Understandable

Definition ....

Example 1 ....

Example 2 ....

d Robust

Definition ....

Example 1 ....

Example 2 ....

Short-answer exam-style practice questions

1 State two responsibilities of the employee when working with display screen equipment (DSE). (2 marks)

  ....

  ....

2 Organisations that collect data about individuals must comply with the Data Protection Act 2018.

  a Explain the purpose of the Data Protection Act, 2018. (2 marks)

  ....

  ....

  b What is a data subject? (1 mark)

  ....

  c Explain two ways in which an organisation can comply with the Data Protection Act, 2018. (4 marks)

  ....

  ....

  ....

  ....

  d Identify two exemptions to the Data Protection Act, 2018. (2 marks)

  ....

  ....

4 Legislation and regulatory requirements

3 Compare the purposes of white hat hackers and a black hat hackers when attacking a digital network. (2 marks)

....

....

> **Hint**
>
> This question is asking for the reasons why two different types of hackers would attack a digital network. The word 'compare' requires you to show clearly that you understand the purpose of each *and* how they differ from one another.

4 A company tracks the delivery of its goods using technology.

   a Explain one way in which the company can track the vehicles used by its staff when delivering the goods. (2 marks)

....

....

   b An employee is contacted by the company to find out why the GPS data is showing that they have not moved for 30 minutes.

   State two reasons why this data could cause issues between the employee and the company. (4 marks)

....

....

....

....

....

....

5 Explain what the ECHR Articles protect. (1 mark)

....

6 Explain consent in marketing. (2 marks)

....

....

7 Define the purpose of the BCS Code of Conduct. (2 marks)

....

....

8 Describe one benefit to a technology company of the IETF. (2 marks)

....

....

Long-answer exam-style practice questions

1 A mobile phone manufacturer is developing a mobile device.

Discuss why the mobile phone manufacturer may want to monitor the electronic communications of its employees in the workplace. (9 marks)

> **Plan your own answer**
>
> To start solving the problem, decompose it (break it down into parts). The first table will help you define the terms used in question 1. The second table will help you construct your answer.
>
> | Key words in the question | How these relate to your answer |
> |---|---|
> | Discuss | |
> | Mobile phone manufacturer | |
> | Monitor electronic communications | |
> | Employees | |
>
> Complete the second table, summarising the points you will cover in your answer. Remember to cover both negative and positive impacts. One impact has been done for you.
>
> | Points to cover | Content to include |
> |---|---|
> | Lack of trust | Workers will not feel trusted if their communications are being monitored, leading to disgruntled employees who might even leave the company, impacting business |
> | | |
> | | |
>
> Now write your answer for question 1 using the information that you have planned.

....

....

4 Legislation and regulatory requirements

2 A solar panel installation company wants a new website which will allow users to book a domestic installation.
   Evaluate the ethical considerations that would need to be addressed in a new code of practice for the company employees due to the new website. (9 marks)

> **Sample answer**
>
> Ethics are the moral principles that a person follows in their behaviour and actions. These are based on what they believe is right. Ethics will affect how a person works and an organisation delivers its services. The new website will require users to enter their personal details and submit them to the company. This will mean that the website will contain a range of form elements, including text boxes, radio buttons and a submit button. These elements must be clear on the screen for users to understand their requirements. The form elements must also be easily usable by those who use a range of adaptive technologies. This will ensure that no potential users are treated unfairly, and all can use the site fully. To help ensure this the web content accessibility guidelines are highlighted in the code of practice and included in-staff training for the company.
>
> Staff in the company should also be trained in how to access and use the data correctly. This would not only allow the company to comply with the Data Protection Act, 2018, but also to ensure that staff are aware of the steps that they should take when using the computer systems and editing the data.
>
> **Comment**
>
> The answer first addresses what ethics are and how this could impact on an organisation in general. This shows an understanding of the topic that is being addressed in the question. The response then goes on to explain how the new website should be accessible to all potential users, regardless of any technologies they use. This is an ethical issue as the company should ensure that all potential users have the same access ability to the content. The response then discusses how this issue could be addressed in the code of practice via the use of WCAG and staff training. This shows an application of knowledge and understanding that is relevant to the context. These points could be expanded on further.
>
> The response also includes a further issue that staff training could cover – access to and editing of data. This is brief and needs further expansion. A good level of knowledge and understanding is shown by referring to the legal issues that the staff training would cover. This demonstrates a good understanding of the complexity of the issues.
>
> Now write your own answer for question 2, making sure you cover these points. No final evaluation is provided.

3   A solar panel installation company wants a new website which will allow users to book domestic panel installation.

Discuss the different legislations that the solar panel installation company will need to comply with when the website is implemented. (12 marks)

....

....

....

....

....

....

....

....

4 Discuss the impact of the World Wide Web Consortium (W3C) on the development of IT systems. (9 marks)

5 Explain how better training of reception staff at a hotel will enhance the security of the data held by the hotel. (9 marks)

6 Discuss how the monitoring of employees in the workplace can have both beneficial and detrimental effects on the employees. (9 marks)

7 Evaluate the impact of professional codes of conduct on the provision of digital services by a solar panel installation company. (9 marks)

5 Business context

Recall activities

1. Copy and complete the table by providing a definition for each sector and three examples of organisations or businesses in the sector, together with the service they provide and a product that they produce.

	Primary sector	Secondary sector	Tertiary sector	Public sector
Definition of the sector				
Examples of organisations or businesses	1 2 3	1 2 3	1 2 3	1 2 3
Examples of services provided	1 2 3	1 2 3	1 2 3	1 2 3
Examples of products produced	1 2 3	1 2 3	1 2 3	1 2 3

2. Describe two ways in which software can be used to manage an inventory.

    1 ....

    2 ....

3. Complete the following sentences.

    A feasibility study is conducted during the ....

    phase of a project. The feasibility study aims to determine if a project is .... or

    not. It will assess whether the project is viable and worth ....

    .... time and .... in. During a feasibility study, the

    project will be assessed to check that it is .... and practically possible using

    the .... available without contravening .... regulations.

4 List two advantages and two disadvantages of carrying out a feasibility study.

Advantages

1 ....

2 ....

Disadvantages

1 ....

2 ....

5 Solve the clues to complete the crossword.

Across

1 Classification of end users based on their abilities to complete tasks
6 Technology should be simplified for use by end users who have a low level of ....
7 Ensuring that all users, irrespective of their physical limitations, can use technology
8 The negative characteristic of the continual evolution of technology used by organisations
10 Fictional characters, based on research, created to represent different types of end users

Down

2 .... audience, the users who are employees of a company
3 The ability for an end user to be online anywhere
4 The opposite of important information
5 The positive characteristic of widespread access to technology when needed
9 The financial burden of resources and tools

6 Complete the table to show how digital technologies can be used in each area to add value to a business. Use examples from a range of different businesses and organisations.

Area	How IT can add value to a business
Overhead costs	
Improving efficiency	
Facilitating growth	
Recruiting talent	

7 Changes in an organisation can come about for three different reasons: developmental, transitional and transformational.

Write a definition of each of these reasons, indicating how they can lead to change in an organisation.

Developmental ....

....

Transitional ....

....

Transformational ....

....

8 Complete the two matrix grids with four examples for each.

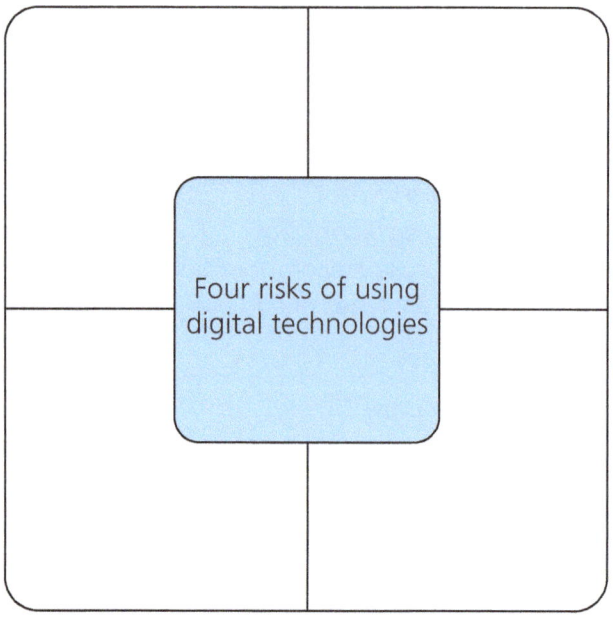

Short-answer exam-style practice questions

1 a Explain which business sector a solar panel manufacturing company is in. (2 marks)

....

....

b Explain two ways in which digital technologies could be used by the solar panel manufacturer for their logistics. (2 marks)

....

....

2 a Explain why a cinema is classed as part of the tertiary sector. (2 marks)

....

....

> **Hint**
>
> The first step is to consider is what a cinema does. Does it create a product or does it provide a service? In this case, no product is produced or created – a cinema allows customers to consume a film. So, therefore, it provides a service.
>
> Step two – what is the tertiary sector? It is the sector that only provides services. Service industries do not actually manufacture anything.
>
> So, the answer that needs to be written should state that a cinema only provides a service (to view a film). The films are produced by other organisations, not by the cinema. This matches the definition of what a tertiary sector industry does.

b Explain two benefits of a cinema using cloud-based technology to handle their ticket sales. (4 marks)

....

....

....

....

c Explain two ways in which the use of cloud-based technologies could increase risk for the cinema. (4 marks)

....

....

....

....

d Explain why good user experience is central to ensuring the cinema delivers a high-quality service. (3 marks)

....

....

....

3 A hospital has decided to introduce a new IT system to store and update patient records. The hospital has employed a project manager.

a Identify and describe two dependencies that the project manager would be responsible for. (2 marks)

....

....

....

b Describe two types of constraints that would be considered in a feasibility study. (2 marks)

....

....

....

....

c Explain how a lack of training for staff could affect the successful implementation of the new system. (2 marks)

....

....

d Identify and explain two measurable values that can be used to add value to an organisation when assessing the importance of digital technologies within an organisation. (2 marks)

....

....

....

Long-answer exam-style practice questions

1. A cinema is planning to use cloud-based technology to handle ticket sales. During discussions about how this should be implemented, several methods are put forward.

   Evaluate whether a parallel or phased method of implementing the change would be beneficial. (9 marks)

   Plan your own answer
   To start solving the problem, decompose it (break it down into parts). The table will help you define the terms used in question 1. Some rows have been done for you. Complete the others.

Points to consider	How this relates to your answer
Evaluate	'Evaluate' means considering strengths and weaknesses of both methods, *and* providing a judgement or conclusion about the best method
Parallel method strengths	Runs alongside existing system Can check performance against existing system Will not lose data, performance or functionality as systems run side by side Issues can be seen and rectified in the new system
Parallel method weaknesses	
Phased method strengths	
Phased method weaknesses	
Context – cloud technology for ticket sales	

Digital Production, Design and Development T Level Exam Practice Workbook

> **Sample answer**
>
> There are two methods of implementation that could be used by the cinema when introducing a new system. Both methods will allow the implementation to be monitored and issues to be fixed during the implementation process.
>
> The first methodology involves implementing the new cloud-based system in parallel with the existing system. This would allow for a direct comparison to be made between the two systems, so ensuring that the new system is matching and then exceeding the existing system. There would be no break in service for the customers as they could still use the existing system and book tickets to see films at the cinema.
>
> However, by running in parallel several issues could develop. The first is the amount of data stored – with two systems running in parallel there would be twice the amount of data. This would put a strain on the storage systems. The duplication of data could also lead to the possibility of increased data errors, which would impact on customer service.
>
> **Comment**
>
> The response starts by setting the context of the question, a cinema and how the methods could be used in general. The response then goes on to look specifically at the use of parallel implementation. The response covers some strengths regarding technical issues and business-related issues, such as maintaining customer services. The response then discusses the weaknesses of using the parallel methodology, such as increased data storage requirements and possible data errors. These are linked to the impact on the customers. The student has effectively applied their knowledge to the context of the question and has started to provide an argument-style response.
>
> This response needs to be developed further by repeating this style of commentary for the other methodology, phased implementation. This would show the application of knowledge to the vocational context of the question.
>
> A final evaluative statement should be made comparing the two methodologies, followed by a recommendation that is suitable for this context.

2 Discuss how rapid changes in technology have had an impact on education in England. (9 marks)

....

....

....

....

....

....

....

....

....

....

....

3 Discuss the benefits and drawbacks of the cinema in question 1 implementing a feasibility study when deciding whether to use cloud-based technology to handle ticket sales. (9 marks)

....

....

....

....

....

....

....

....

....

....

4 Evaluate the impact of zero-day vulnerabilities on the implementation of a new digital tracking system by a transport company. (9 marks)

....

....

....

....

....

....

....

....

....

....

> **Hint**
>
> Start with what you know or can find out easily. Think specifically about a real-world transport company that you can research. How does this business use a digital tracking system?
>
> Next, research the term 'zero-day vulnerability'. What does this mean for digital systems in general? What are the issues that can be caused? Apply what you found out to the real-world company you researched to help you write your answer.

5 Explain how the risk of operational disruption increases when introducing new digital technologies. (9 marks)

....

6 A local car hire company has commissioned a new application that will automatically calculate customer fees for vehicle rentals.

Compare the impact of two constraints on the success of the implementation of the project. (9 marks)

....

7 Evaluate how the documentation of a change process is a key part of implementing a new digital system. (9 marks)

8 Evaluate how the use of new digital technologies can affect the reputation of a transport company. (9 marks)

6 Data

Recall activities

1. Complete the information relationship diagram.

    data + [..............................] + [..............................] + meaning

2. Complete the table defining the terminology.

Term	Definition
Data	
Information	
Knowledge	
Quantitative data	
Qualitative data	

3. List six reasons why an organisation needs to use data.

    1 ....
    2 ....
    3 ....
    4 ....
    5 ....
    6 ....

4. Data is generated in several ways. For each of the methods listed here, provide two examples of how data is generated.

    Human generated

    Example 1 ....
    Example 2 ....

    Transactional data

    Example 1 ....
    Example 2 ....

    Sensors

    Example 1 ....
    Example 2 ....

5 Create a mind map of the different data types and include two examples for each type of data in the diagram.

6 Complete the following paragraph.

Data wrangling is the .... of .... raw data into a more usable and .... form. Data wrangling can help .... data for ...., visualisation, or machine ....

7 Complete the six steps involved in data wrangling. Two have been done for you.

1 Discovery

2 ....

3 ....

4 ....

5 ....

6 Output

8 a The purpose of which information tool is to gather, analyse, process and report data?

....

b Which tool is used for activities such as planning and setting budgets, budget forecasting and modelling?

....

c Which tool is used to make customer-facing employee's work easier and less time consuming?

....

9 Complete the diagram.

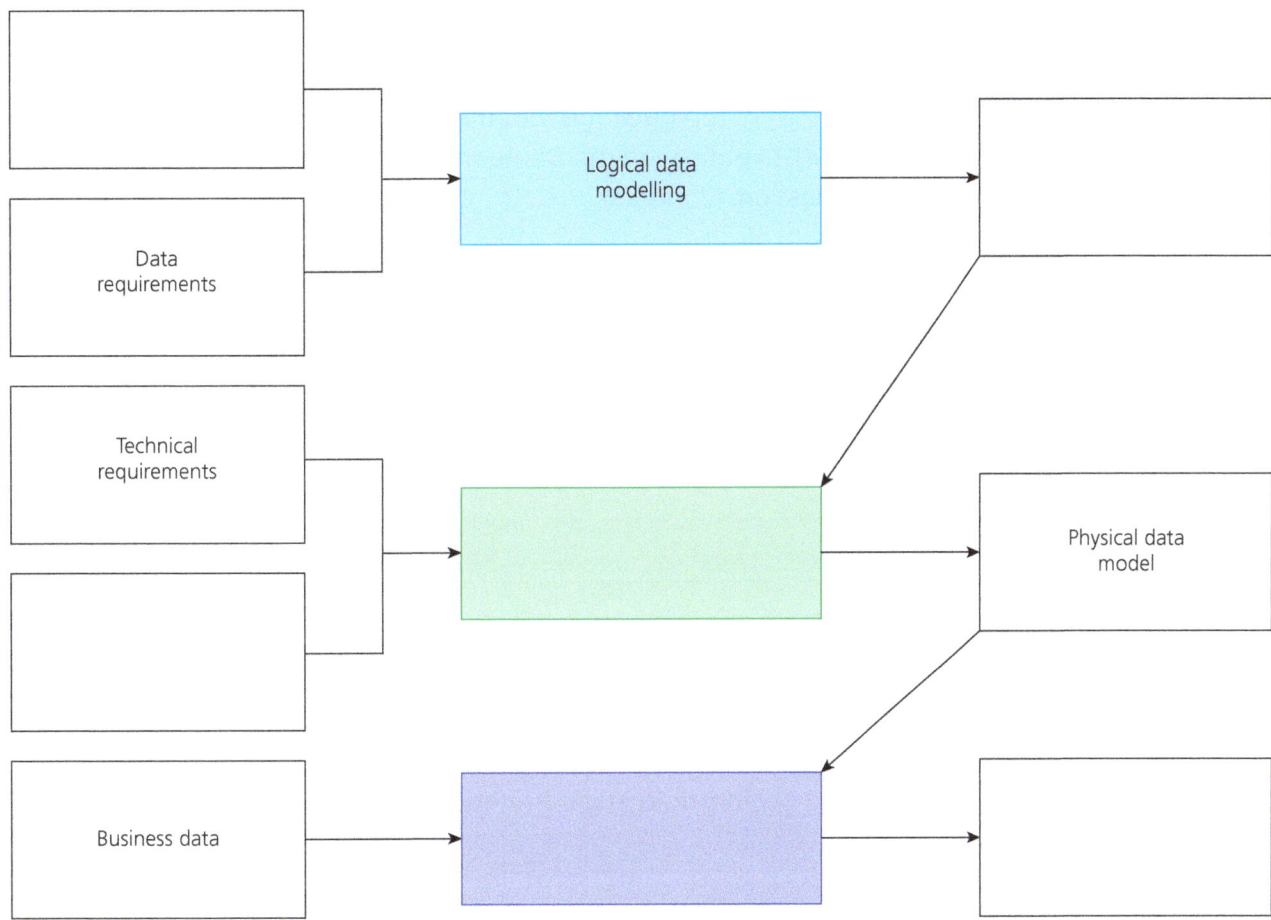

10 List and define the six Vs.

V	Definition

11 Explain the purposes of the following data analysis tools.

Data warehousing ....

Data lakes ....

Data mining ....

Data reporting ....

Digital Production, Design and Development T Level Exam Practice Workbook

Short-answer exam-style practice questions

1 A shipping company has a website for customers to book collections and deliveries of packages.

   a When customers enter the details of the package that they want to send, they can choose if they want to schedule a pickup. Explain why the Boolean data type is most appropriate to provide a response for this question. (2 marks)

   ....

   ....

   b When customers book a pickup, they enter the number of packages to be collected, with a short description of each package. List and explain which data provided by the customer is qualitative and which is quantitative. (2 marks)

   Qualitative data ....

   ....

   Quantitative data ....

   ....

   c Scanners are used to register each package at various points through the journey, from collection to delivery. Explain how this data is generated using the scanner. (2 marks)

   ....

   ....

   d Explain why the collection and delivery of packages can be classified as transactional data. (2 marks)

   ....

   ....

   e The data generated is stored in a file-based structure. Explain why a file-based structure is used to store the data. (2 marks)

   ....

   ....

   f When the collections and deliveries are scheduled for the day, a digital report is provided to each driver. Explain why a digital report is provided to each driver. (2 marks)

   ....

   ....

> **Hint**
>
> First, consider the nature of a digital report and what would it contain. Second, state why it would be needed.

Photocopying prohibited

2 A supermarket is developing a loyalty card scheme which will record what customers buy and send them special offers based on their past purchases.

   a During the development of the system, a data warehouse is created.

   Explain the purpose of a data warehouse. (2 marks)

   ....

   ....

   b The supermarket wants to use data mining on the data collected from the new loyalty card scheme.

   Define the term 'data mining' and explain why the supermarket would use it with their new system. (2 marks)

   ....

   ....

   ....

   c Define an API. (2 marks)

   ....

   ....

   d The data stored in the loyalty card scheme contains metadata.

   Using an example from the supermarket loyalty card scheme, describe what administrative metadata is. (2 marks)

   ....

   ....

   e Explain how the use of administrative metadata will allow the supermarket loyalty card scheme to comply with appropriate regulatory requirements. (2 marks)

   ....

   ....

Long-answer exam-style practice questions

1 A supermarket is developing a loyalty card scheme which will record what customers buy and send them special offers based on their past purchases.

   Discuss the use of APIs in the loyalty card scheme system. Your discussion should include:

   ▷ the benefits and drawbacks of using APIs

   ▷ a conclusion. (9 marks)

Plan your own answer

To start solving the problem, decompose it (break it down into parts). The table will help you define the terms used in question 1. Some rows have been done for you. Complete the others.

Points to consider	How does it relate to your answer?
Discuss	'Discuss' means considering both aspects of a point of view. This question requires discussion of benefits *and* drawbacks of using APIs.
Define an API	This is a computer program that allows access to and use of data on different platforms.
Benefit of APIs	
Drawbacks of APIs	
Loyalty card scheme	
How the scheme be accessed by CUSTOMERS	
How the scheme will be accessed by SUPERMARKET	

....

....

....

....

....

....

....

....

....

....

....

....

....

....

2 Discuss how the supermarket managers from question 1 will be able to use the data collected to inform their decision making. (9 marks)

> **Sample answer**
>
> The loyalty card scheme will collect details about shoppers at the supermarket. This will include data about who they are, from their account details, and what they buy. The supermarket can then create a picture of what their customers are buying. The supermarket can alter the stock to suit the customers.
>
> The supermarket will be able to make strategic decisions about what to sell over the long term. This means that the supermarket's buyers can contact suppliers and order the stock early and in bulk. This could save money that could be passed onto customers.
>
> The supermarket will also know what products people are not buying. If customers are not purchasing certain products, then the supermarket can stop selling them. This would save money and prevent waste. In the long term, this would allow the supermarket to be more profitable.
>
> **Comment**
>
> This response starts off talking about what data could be collected through the loyalty card scheme and how the data could be used. The response should specifically mention that operational decisions are made based on the data collected.
>
> The response discusses how the data can be used for strategic decision making, covering the impact on the business and customers. This could be expanded with specific examples, provided they fit the context. The answer goes on to talk about using data to reduce stock levels. This again could be expanded on with specific examples, e.g. suncream not selling in winter.
>
> The answer needs to be developed further to enter the highest marking level, by using specific examples to help illustrate the points made.

3 A shipping company has a website for customers to book collections and deliveries of packages. Explain why a JSON data format could be used with the system. (9 marks)

....

4 Explain how data can be used to monitor the use of a news organisation's website and enhance the service provided. (9 marks)

....

6 Data

5 Discuss how the data generated by a customer using a shipping company's website to book a package collection moves through the three states of data: at rest, in use and in motion.
(9 marks)

6 Discuss how a large online retailer would use data analysis tools to improve their products and sales. (9 marks)

7 Evaluate the use of the six Vs when assessing the quality of data held in a big data set.
(9 marks)

7 Digital environments

Recall activities

1 Complete the table to give characteristics and uses of digital devices.

Computer system	Three characteristics	Three uses
Mobile device	1 2 3	1 2 3
Personal computer	1 2 3	1 2 3
Server	1 2 3	1 2 3
Smart device	1 2 3	1 2 3

2 Define the purpose each of the following types of software.

Batch OS ....

....

Multi-tasking/time-sharing OS ....

....

Real time OS ....

....

Network OS ....

....

Mobile OS ....

....

Utility software ....

....

Photocopying prohibited 71

3 a Which tool allows code to be written and updated?

....

b Which tool tests code, highlighting errors?

....

c Which tool converts low level programming code into machine code?

....

d Which tool provides a central interface for a developer to access different programming tools?

....

4 Explain these terms.

a Redundancy ....

....

b Data striping ....

....

c Parity ....

....

d Mirroring ....

....

e RAID ....

....

f NAS ....

....

g SAN ....

....

5 Complete the word search based on the questions provided. Write each answer next to the question when you have found it.

```
L N D R K E C R R O C P I
O O S M W M L L H H L O W
S B A N D W I D T H F I M
Y D T D P Y I A S E N A L
M L E E B I O A N A C A B
N S C A L A B I L I T Y G
G S T E A O L H N E T S E
A I F I U N Y A N S E T O
R T S I H D T C N R U O C
A U N B H O Y E V C G A H
Q A C I T P O E R B I F S
R R O U T E R N R P T N H
J D E O N R T T E L F D G
```

1 Ability to increase or decrease size if needed

....

2 Movement of demand to different parts of a network where there are spare resources

....

3 Measure of time taken to transmit data from one point to another on a network

....

4 Unique address coded on each NIC that identifies the device

....

5 The informal address of a local network

....

6 Central device that can be used for storage, applications and print management

....

7 Fastest method of wired connection for a network

....

8 Group of computers and devices connected over a short distance

....

9 The measurement of how much data can be transferred from one point of a network to another in a specified time scale

....

10 Device responsible for forwarding data to their intended IP addresses

....

Digital Production, Design and Development T Level Exam Practice Workbook

6 Explain one difference between a logical and physical network topology.

....

....

7 Summarise the role of each of these components in a network.

Server ....

....

ISPs ....

....

Router ....

....

Network switch ....

....

Client ....

8 Complete the diagram by adding in the layer and protocols included.

7	Application	Upper layers	
6			JPEG, MIDI, MPEG
5			
4		Lower layers	
3			IP, PIX, RIP, ARP, ICMP, RARP, EGP, NetBEUI, DLC
2			
1			No protocols

9 Complete the diagram by adding in the layer and protocols included.

4		Telnet, FTP, SMTP, DNS, RIP, NMP
3		
2		
1		Ethernet, Token ring, Frame relay, ATM

74 **Photocopying prohibited**

10 List three benefits and three limitations of virtual environments.

Benefits

1 ....
....

2 ....
....

3 ....
....

Limitations

1 ....
....

2 ....
....

3 ....
....

11 Define the cloud-computing delivery models.

a IaaS stands for ....
....

b PaaS stands for ....
....

c SaaS stands for ....
....

d DaaS stands for ....
....

12 What is a subscriber?
....
....

13 What is a service provider?
....
....

14 What are dashboards?

....

....

15 Identify two benefits and two limitations of using each of these methods.

  a Data and system redundancy

  Benefits

  1 ....

  2 ....

  Limitations

  1 ....

  2 ....

  b Back-up systems

  Benefits

  1 ....

  2 ....

  Limitations

  1 ....

  2 ....

  c Hot, cold and warm sites

  Benefits

  1 ....

  2 ....

  Limitations

  1 ....

  2 ....

  d Data back-up and recovery procedures

  Benefits

  1 ....

  2 ....

  Limitations

  1 ....

  2 ....

7 Digital environments

e Device hardening

Benefits

1 ....

2 ....

Limitations

1 ....

2 ....

Short-answer exam-style practice questions

1 a The diagram shows an office network.

Identify the components labelled A–D. (2 marks)

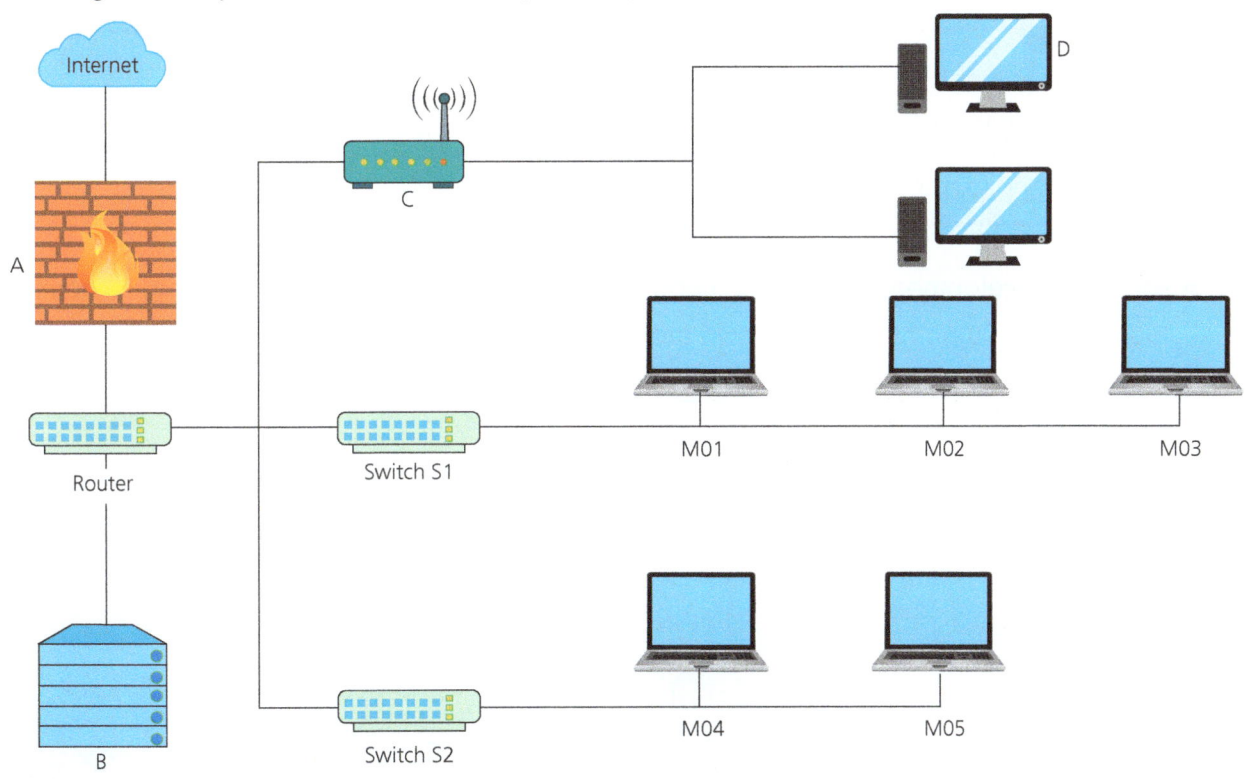

A ....

B ....

C ....

D ....

b Explain the purpose of a switch. (2 marks)

....

2 a Describe two limitations of using mobile devices when working away from the office. (2 marks)

....

....

b Identify two input devices that are integrated into mobile devices. For each device describe one use in the office context. (2 marks)

....

....

c Explain the role of a mobile operating system. (2 marks)

....

....

> **Hint**
> This question asks you to think about what devices are used to enter data into a computer system in an office. However, it asks only about mobile devices, such as smart phones, tablets and laptops.

3 A software development company is setting up a new data storage and recovery system.

a Identify which type of RAID is shown the diagram. (1 mark)

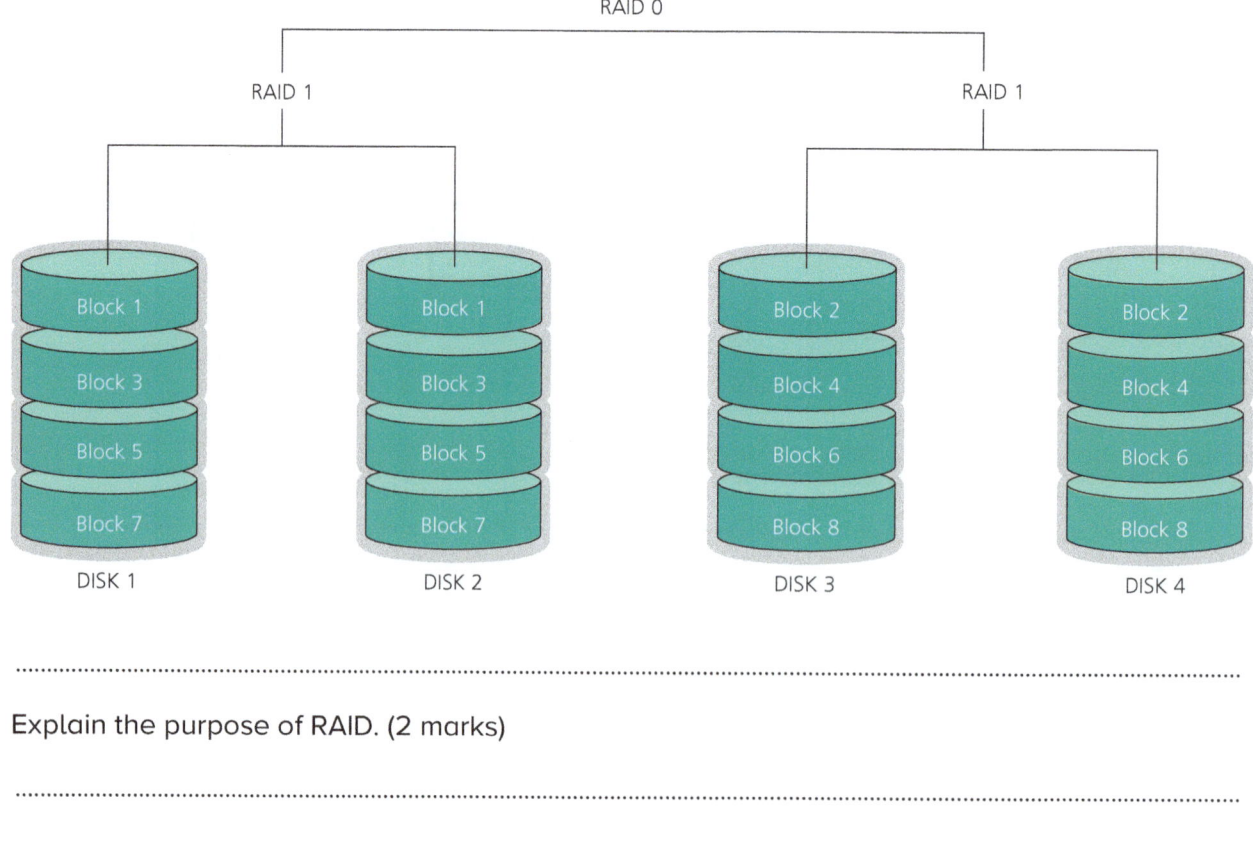

....

b Explain the purpose of RAID. (2 marks)

....

....

c RAID uses multiple disk drives in a single array to store data. Explain one way that data striping is different to mirroring. (2 marks)

....

....

....

d Explain two drawbacks of connecting devices together to form a network. (2 marks)

....

....

....

4 A software development company is moving to a multi-floor building and is installing a network that covers the whole building.

a Explain one function of the application layer in the seven-layer OSI model. (2 marks)

....

....

....

b Explain one function of the network layer in the seven-layer OSI model. (2 marks)

....

....

....

> **Hint**
>
> First identify one function of the network layer, then expand it by explaining its impact in the OSI model.

c Data will be stored on the cloud. Explain the purpose of the FTP protocol. (2 marks)

....

....

....

d Identify three protocols in the transport OSI layer. (3 marks)

1 ....

2 ....

3 ....

5 A market research company is streamlining the IT systems that it uses. It is considering developing a virtual environment to carry out tasks.

  a Explain data virtualisation. (2 marks)

  b Explain one reason why data virtualisation would be appropriate for a market research company. (2 marks)

  c Explain one reason why the company should adopt server virtualisation. (2 marks)

  d Explain the role of a hypervisor in a virtual environment. (2 marks)

6 A car hire firm has installed a new digital system so it can monitor all the vehicles that it owns. The main office is currently located away from the garages where the vehicles are stored.

  a Explain one reason why using a cloud-computing system would benefit the car hire company. (2 marks)

  b Explain two reasons why the company should adopt a SaaS model of cloud computing. (2 marks)

  c Describe what performance metrics are in cloud computing. (2 marks)

7 Digital environments

Long-answer exam-style practice questions

1 A college with multiple campus sites is installing a VLAN.

   Discuss the benefits and limitations of the college installing and using a VLAN. (9 marks)

   ....
   ....
   ....
   ....
   ....
   ....
   ....
   ....
   ....
   ....
   ....

   > **Hint**
   >
   > First, consider what a VLAN is and how could multiple campuses use VLANs within one network. Does splitting a network up into VLANs based on the different campuses appear to be logical? Next, weigh up the benefits and limitations of installing and using a VLAN.

2 Evaluate the use of a tree or mesh network when developing a school network. (9 marks)

   > **Plan your own answer**
   >
   > To start solving the problem, decompose it (break it down into parts). The table will help you define the terms used in question 2.
   >
   > | Points to consider | How these relate to your answer |
   > |---|---|
   > | Evaluate | |
   > | Tree network | |
   > | Benefits | |
   > | Drawbacks | |
   > | Mesh network | |
   > | Benefits | |
   > | Drawbacks | |
   > | Context: School network | |

Sample answer

A tree network allows existing systems to be expanded relatively easily. This is important in a school context as the school probably has an existing network that is being developed. A tree network allows new parts to be added to the existing one. New buildings can be added to the existing network without too much disruption to the network as a whole. However, if one node of the network breaks, then all those areas that are built off that node will be inaccessible. There is an increased risk of this happening if a new network section is added to an existing network.

A mesh network would allow for direct cabling between all the aspects of the network. This would reduce data traffic conflicts as dedicated connections would be used. However, the cost of installing a mesh network could be high. Significant cabling would be required on a school site to connect all the necessary locations directly together. There may be issues installing the cable due to the nature of the building structures.

Comment

This response talks about both types of networks: tree and mesh. Benefits and weaknesses of both types are covered. The response contains information related to the specific context of the question – explaining how a school could be impacted by the two different types of networks. This shows a good application of knowledge and understanding to the context. To access the highest marks, the points made should be developed further clearly indicating the impact on the school context.

3 Evaluate the introduction into a cinema of internet-enabled devices for customer ordering. (9 marks)

4 When purchasing a new laptop for work, discuss the different types of secondary devices that should be considered. (9 marks)

5 Evaluate the installation of a thin client network in a university. (9 marks)

....

....

....

....

....

....

....

....

....

....

....

....

....

6 Discuss the benefits and limitations of setting up a client–server network in a hospital setting. (9 marks)

....

....

....

....

....

....

....

....

....

....

....

....

....

7 Evaluate the use of wireless networks in a retail park. (9 marks)

....

....

....

....

....

....

....

....

....

....

....

....

....

....

8 Evaluate the use of DaaS cloud-based computing by a market research company. (9 marks)

....

....

....

....

....

....

....

....

....

....

....

....

....

....

9 Discuss how redundancy must be considered when developing a new digital system for a car hire firm. (9 marks)

....

10 Discuss the benefits and limitations of using a wired network in a food storage warehouse. (9 marks)

....

8 Security

Recall activities

1. Define these key terms.

   Privacy ....

   Confidentiality ....

   Vulnerabilities ....

2. Read the descriptions in the table and identify the technical threat or vulnerability.

Description of context	Technical threat or vulnerability
Network of private computers that hackers have infected with malicious software that is controlled remotely	
Interface between software applications that lack up to date security measures	
Network of computers used to flood a targeted server or network with excess traffic	
Network that allows individual devices to communicate directly with each other	
Unauthorised access to a digital system	
The interception of data between two devices by a hacker who places themselves in the middle of the communication channel	
A piece of software designed specifically to steal data, damage or destroy a digital system	
The art of manipulating people to find out information leading to a digital compromise	

3. Fill in each box with a definition for each part of the CIA triangle and state how it improves information security.

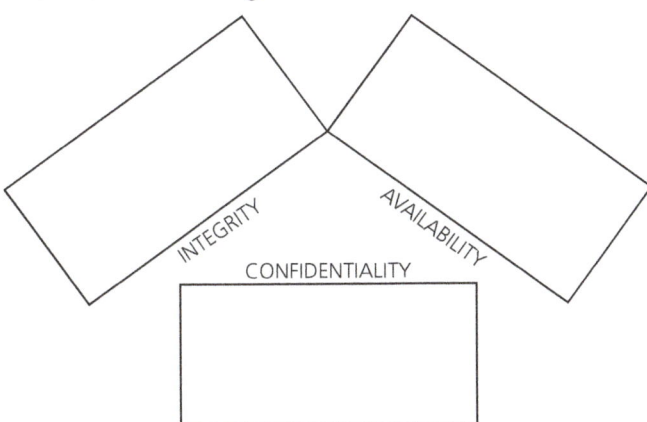

Photocopying prohibited   87

4 Complete the paragraph.

The aim of digital security is to protect .... systems together with the .... and information that they hold. By applying .... measures to a digital system, the chances that a threat will be successful is .... This is because the .... to a system, human, ... and technical have been .... This has then led to .... being put in place that .... those chances of the vulnerabilities being compromised. The application of security to a digital system helps ensure that the .... triad is maintained.

5 Complete the table to identify mitigation measures that could be used to prevent each threat. Each threat may have more than one possible mitigation.

Threat	Mitigation method
Accidental data modification by a junior member of staff	
Attempted theft of company plans by external individual	
Attempted theft of money from an online bank account	
Interception of communications	
Damage to digital system through flooding	
Ransomware attack on stored data	

Short-answer exam-style practice questions

1 A software development company has one network in its offices.

   a Identify three examples of employee data that must be kept confidential. (3 marks)

   1 ....

   2 ....

   3 ....

   b Explain one financial cost to the company if the data is not kept confidential. (2 marks)

   ....

   ....

   c The company has recently restructured, involving some job losses.

   Identify and describe one possible human threat to the company's computer system. (2 marks)

   ....

   ....

   d Explain one mitigation that could be implemented to reduce this human threat. (2 marks)

   ....

   ....

2 A car hire firm has an app that allows customers to use their own devices when booking and returning hire cars.

   a Explain the role of APIs in the hire firm's system. (2 marks)

   ....

   ....

   b Describe one vulnerability that using APIs could cause. (2 marks)

   ....

   ....

   c Identify and describe one other possible technical vulnerability that could occur by allowing customers to use their own devices. (2 marks)

   ....

   ....

> **Hint**
>
> This question asks for a technical vulnerability caused by customers using their own devices to access the app. Read the question carefully as it asks for another vulnerability *in addition* to using APIs.

3 A market research company allows staff to work from home and in the office.

   a When staff work from home, they use a VPN to access the company's systems.

   Explain one reason for using an VPN for this purpose. (2 marks)

   ....

   ....

   b When logging into a company system, employees are required to use multi-factor authentication (MFA).

   Explain two advantages of using MFA. (2 marks)

   ....

   ....

   c Explain one reason why employees are required to change their password for the company system every 90 days. (2 marks)

   ....

   ....

4 A supermarket runs a loyalty card scheme which records customer purchases and uses the data to send tailored special offers.

   a Explain two external human threats to the customer data. (2 marks)

   ....

   ....

   b The supermarket employs an external company to test their system.

   Explain penetration testing. (2 marks)

   ....

   ....

   c Identify two types of penetration testing. (2 marks)

   ....

   ....

8 Security

Long-answer exam-style practice questions

1 A supermarket runs a loyalty card scheme which records customer purchases and uses the data to send tailored special offers.

Discuss the possible technical threats to this loyalty card scheme system. (9 marks)

Plan your own answer

To start solving the problem, decompose it (break it down into parts). The table walks you through the steps you need to take to answer question 1. Some advice has been provided.

Points to consider	How these relate to your answer
Command word	
Context	Think about real-world examples of customer loyalty card schemes
Technical threats	

2. A food delivery firm is updating its booking system to include an app that customers can use to order meals.

Evaluate the risk from DDoS attacks on the system and discuss the mitigations that could be implemented to reduce the chances of a successful DDoS attack. (9 marks)

> **Sample answer**
>
> A DDoS attack aims to prevent or reduce access to a computer system that is used by a business. The aim is to disrupt the business, in this case a food delivery firm. A DDoS attack is carried out by flooding the server with requests from many devices. This is possible as the app will be installed on multiple customers' phones. Each device has a copy of the app that could be used to connect to the system. The potential for installing and using an app on many devices is high.
>
> One method of reducing the chance of a successful DDoS attack is by using SYN cookies. In this case, the booking system would wait for a specific response including an ACK packet from the user app and would, only then, create a connection that could be used to complete the food ordering process. Requests with no ACK packet would be timed out, reducing the request demands on the system and so reducing the chance of a successful DDoS attack.

8 Security

> **Comment**
> This response starts by explaining what a DDoS attack is and what it aims to do. The response then links this to the risk of the app being used to create a DDoS attack. The response talks about the fact that the app is on many separate devices, increasing the possible number of requests. This could, in turn, lead to a DDoS attack. The answer could be expanded to explain in more detail about how the flood of requests could impact the system – the last sentence in paragraph one is very brief.
>
> The response then talks about a possible mitigation method and how this would reduce the chance of a DDoS attack being successful. This method shows a sound technical understanding of one mitigation method.
>
> This response would be placed towards the top of level 2. To gain higher marks, the response should be expanded as suggested and should also cover more mitigation methods that would work alongside the method already mentioned.

3 A car hire firm has suffered a cyberattack resulting in customer data being stolen.

Discuss the impact on the car hire firm of the theft of the customer data. (9 marks)

....
....
....
....
....
....
....
....
....
....
....
....
....
....

> **Hint**
> This question is about the impact on the car hire firm, not the customers. So, while the effect on the customers would be considered in so far as these also affect the company, the marks are awarded for the impact on the car hire firm. Talking about customer identity theft is not relevant as that's an impact on the customer. The impact on the car hire firm is that they will suffer financially in a number of ways.

4 A food delivery firm is updating its booking system to include an app that customers can use to order and pay for meals.

Discuss the security measures that should be included to protect data in the system. (9 marks)

....

....

....

....

....

....

....

....

....

....

....

....

5 A local supermarket runs a loyalty card scheme which records customer purchases. The data is stored on a server in the offices at the back of the shop.

Evaluate the physical vulnerabilities to the data and possible mitigation measures. (9 marks)

....

....

....

....

....

....

....

....

....

....

....

....

6 Following a cyberattack, a car hire firm has updated its security policies and procedures.

Discuss the role of policy enforcement and training in implementing the new policies and procedures. (9 marks)

DIGITAL PRODUCTION, DESIGN & DEVELOPMENT: CORE
EXAM PRACTICE WORKBOOK

Develop the vital skills you need to achieve your best in the T Level exams with this accessible and engaging Exam Practice Workbook.

- Review and consolidate your knowledge, with varied recall activities for every topic including crosswords, quizzes and more
- Reinforce your understanding and boost your exam confidence with both short- and long-answer exam-style practice questions, to help you break down the question
- Improve your exam technique with guidance on how to plan and review your responses, plus exam hints and sample student answers

Also available:

9781398346789 Digital Production, Design and Development T Level: Core
9781398384507 My Revision Notes: Digital Production, Design and Development T Level

'T-LEVELS' is a registered trade mark of the Department for Education.

'T Level' is a registered trade mark of the Institute for Apprenticeships and Technical Education.

The T Level Technical Qualification is a qualification approved and managed by the Institute for Apprenticeships and Technical Education.

HODDER Education
+44 (0)1235 827827
education@hachette.co.uk
www.hoddereducation.com

ISBN 978-1-0360-0699-0